GW00643999

Patrick R. McGrath 111 — the very name su[ggests a] magnate, presiding over a multinational conglo[merate in] Chicago. This is ironic, since Patrick is in fact a s[ingle man] from Bolton. Purely by coincidence, there are 110 [people of the] same name in the Bolton area, and since Patrick was the last to register with the Bolton *Handyman's Gazette*, he's been known ever since as Patrick R. McGrath 111. He's available for jobs both large and small, and has a 24-hour answering service on Bolton 326918 — ring now and he'll answer in about 24 hours' time.

Ian Moore has been contributing articles about money to the *Economist* for years — much to the *Economist*'s annoyance . . . I mean, the last thing they want is to be flooded with unsolicited material from people they've never heard of. That's the trouble with Ian — he never knows when to give up. If you want confirmation of this just ask his wife and seven children . . . no, I tell a lie — eight. He made a lot of money in the Sixties when he was employed by the Royal Mint where he was captain of the Royal Mint Polo team. In the Seventies he got into property — but was caught by the police and charged with burglary.

Peter Fincham is a distinguished essayist, thinker and writer. Among his novels are *Sons and Lovers* by D. H. Lawrence, *Ulysses* by James Joyce and a complete set of Daphne du Maurier. Unfortunately the rest of his book collection was stolen in a recent burglary (the police are questioning Ian Moore in connection with this). Peter's face is well-known in money circles since he looks like the Queen. Although not well off himself he's never slow to put his hand in his pocket and leave it there for days. To date he has written 2 books, 3 cheques and 500 IOUs.

Illustrated by Nigel Paige

Money
MADE SILLY

Patrick R. McGrath 111, Peter Fincham and Ian Moore
CENTURY · LONDON

Also available
Sex Made Silly
Food Made Silly
Skiing Made Silly

Design/Gwyn Lewis
Graphics/Ian Sandom

First published in Great Britain in 1985
by Century Hutchinson Ltd, Brookmount House,
62–65 Chandos Place, Covent Garden, London WC2N 4NW

ISBN 0 7126 1018 9

Filmset by Deltatype, Ellesmere Port
Printed in Great Britain in 1985 by
Hazell, Watson & Viney Ltd., Aylesbury, Bucks

Introduction

As any schoolboy will tell you, the Bible describes money as 'the root of all evil'.

Of course, any schoolboy would be wrong, because the Bible says that 'the *love* of money is the root of all evil'.

Or more exactly Timothy says so. Or rather St Paul says so in his first letter to Timothy. . . . We simply don't know what Timothy himself thought about the love of money, or about anything for that matter.

Like everybody else Paul wrote to — the Romans, the Hebrews, the Corinthians — Timothy was a poor correspondent and never wrote back.

But I digress . . . as I say, the *love* of money is the root of all evil.

(That is, if you accept what it says in the Bible as gospel.)

What is clear is that over the centuries dealings in money have led to lying, cheating, dishonesty, double-dealing and corruption (see *accountancy*).

In *Money Made Silly* we'll be looking at money from a number of different angles, studying it, analysing it and addressing ourselves to important and searching questions, such as 'What is money for?' . . . 'Could we do without it?' . . . and, most pertinently, 'How much are we getting for writing this book?'

Just How Rich

Wealth and poverty are very difficult to define in absolute terms. What is rich? (Dundee cake). What is poor? (*The Little & Large Show*).

It's very easy to be subjective. It's also very easy to wink with alternate eyes. What I find difficult is raising one eyebrow. The only way I can manage it is to raise them both and hold one down.

But I digress . . . now *there*'s something that's very easy . . . aren't Oxford United doing well this season? . . .

Anyway, here's the *Money Made Silly* quiz. Answer the questions on the next page to find out whether you are a rich man, a poor man, a beggarman — or an estate agent.

Are You . . . ?

(1) Are you . . . ?
    (a) Filling in the answers yourself.
    (b) Paying someone to do it for you.

(2) In a restaurant do you check the bill . . . ?
    (a) Never
    (b) Sometimes
    (c) Always, you jillock — I'm the waiter.

(3) In pubs do you . . . ?
    (a) Stand a round
    (b) Stand around until someone else does.

(4) Are you reading this book because   ?
    (a) You've bought it
    (b) It was given to you
    (c) You've bought it to give to someone else so you might as well read it before you give it away.

(5) If a tramp stops you in the street and asks you for money, do you . . . ?
    (a) Give him some
    (b) Have him arrested for begging
    (c) Tell him to get off your patch.

Answers

Write your answers on the back of a £5 note and send it to the authors, who will write back and tell you how they spent it.

(6) If you found a £10 note in the pub would you . . . ?
    (a) Give it to the publican
    (b) Give it to the police
    (c) Spend it first to make sure it was real.

(7) Are you . . . ?
    (a) More generous than average
    (b) About as generous as average
    (c) Less generous than average
    (d) Scottish.

Money · Past, Present and Future

Strange to say in these days of compound interest rates, VAT returns, cash dispensers and galloping inflation, but there was a time when Man did not enjoy the advantages of money.

Students of such things put the 'Time without money' as either just before the last Ice Age, or four weeks after their last grant cheque arrived.

In these early days the only way of getting your hands on the simple necessities of life was by beating up your neighbours or indulging in a spot of friendly bartering.

Bartering was a fantastically simple concept:

'I have too much fish. You have too many potatoes.'
'I give you fish. You give me potatoes.'
'Now I have too many potatoes. You have too much fish.'

This straight swapping was OK, but it did have its drawbacks. If you lived in, say, a mining area, you tended to find yourself with quite a lot of coal on your hands. But if you tried to swap it, you soon found that everyone else for miles around was trying to swap coal as well.

And there was no way you could catch a bus and take your bags of coal to, say, a wheat-producing area . . . because you didn't have anything to pay your bus fare with.

Eventually an enterprising caveman came up with the concept of money.

'This is great,' he thought. 'It will make my fortune — whatever that is.'

Those were great days for inventions. No sooner had

someone invented paper than someone else thought of fire and used up all the paper to start one. Then there was the wheel. The sceptics shook their heads over this manifestly useless object, unable to predict the chain of events that would lead one day to the hostess trolley and the Sinclair C5.

Indeed, some scholars think that it was the same person who invented money as invented the wheel, irritated at the fact that he was never going to be able to collect all the royalties he was due.

Again the sceptics had their doubts.

'I hae ma doubts,' said one, unaccountably doing a Miss Jean Brodie impression.

'This money business,' said another. 'It's all very well. But how much will it cost?'

'Let's put it this way,' said the inventor. 'In the old days it would have cost any amount of coal, fish, cattle and potatoes. But with my new invention we'll be able to work out the cost exactly.'

'Oh brilliant. You've invented something called money which is a method of calculating how much the invention of money will cost us. I thought your bloody wheel thing was a disaster, but this "money" takes the biscuit . . . whatever that is.'

'Eureka! The Wagon Wheel! A biscuit shaped like a wheel which costs money. Oh boy — am I cooking with gas today . . .'

As I say, those were great days for inventions.

Things developed. For a time it was customary to make 'coins' out of valuable metals like silver and gold. Then the trend was to get rid of the valuable metals and use cheap substitutes instead.

This was known as forgery or government policy, depending on who was doing it.

A further step consisted of replacing coins with paper notes, and then getting rid of these as well and going over to a 'cashless society' (e.g. Mexico) where credit cards, charge cards, computer transactions etc. replace actual tokens.

In this so-called cashless society bank robberies and street muggings should become a thing of the past, but nipping out to the corner shop late at night when the computer is down will be rather difficult.

Experts predict, however, that shopkeepers will be prepared to 'sell' their goods in exchange for valuable items that the shopper brings with him.

This ultra-sophisticated system will be called 'bartering'.

Discovering an Oil Well . . .

The oil business has certainly created some of the most fabulously wealthy people in history, e.g. the stars of *Dallas*.

The most famous oil billionaire of all must be J. Paul Getty, who also gained a reputation for being incredibly stingey with his cash. In fact, he even installed a pay phone in his country mansion to discourage his guests from phoning home and telling their friends how mean he was.

Most people associate oil with the Middle East, which until recently was a poor, undeveloped region in which the quality of life had hardly changed since the Middle Ages — a bit like some of the rougher areas of Glasgow.

Now money pours into the region like . . . well, like oil. In other respects things haven't changed so much. In some Middle Eastern states, the law remains a savage instrument of retribution.

If you steal someone's property you can have your hand cut off . . . if you trample somebody to death you can have your feet cut off . . . and if you electrocute somebody you can have your electricity cut off.

£££££££££££££££££££££££

Status Symbols

Status symbols were invented in the Sixties by journalists to describe the possessions of people who were better off than them . . . and let's face it, who isn't?

WORK OF ART   A painting by an old master over your mantelpiece could reasonably be described as a status symbol. Owning a work of art gives you a stake in the priceless cultural heritage of this country, and is also likely to be a good investment. The only trouble is that it will cost a fortune to insure and if authentic will be very ugly to look at with all those fat women, faded colours and dead kings.

COCAINE   'God's way of telling you that you have too much money.'
           This overrated and overpriced drug is much beloved by
           the trendies. It has a number of drawbacks:
           (1) It dissolves your nose
           (2) It involves a lot of surreptitious visits to the lavatory
           (3) Few people can afford the expense of buying endless
               quantities of Bic biros.

CAVIAR   Overrated and overpriced (see *cocaine*, *Starlight Express*,
           file-o-fax, any book by Jeffrey Archer).

ROLLS ROYCE Rolls and Royce met quite by chance in a telephone directory
           nearly a hundred years ago. They produced a car of
           excellence, the envy of the world. The engine is so quiet that
           you can be run over by one without even noticing it.

CARTIER WATCH Often known as the 'Rolls Royce of watches'.

MERCEDES BENZ Often known as the 'Rolls Royce of motor cars'.

PORSCHE   An ugly German car which seats one and a half people
           uncomfortably. Capable of getting from 0 to 60 in the time it
           took Hitler to annex Poland.

SWIMMING   A container, to impress your friends, in which you can
POOL   marinate dead leaves overnight in blue piss.

AU-PAIR   See *divorce*.

DIVORCE   See *au-pair*.

Trouble at T'Pit

Money Made Silly is pleased to present an exclusive extract from a play by middle-class Cambridge graduate Edward Hare about a world he knows so well . . . life in a Northern mining community, with its gross social injustices, its grim, bitter dourness, its dour, bitter grimness, and the endless strife between the rich and the poor, the haves and the have-nots, and those who have but speak in a high pitched voice anyway.

In this extract the workers at the pithead gate confront their boss.

SCENE: FACTORY GATE. MEN IN CLOTH CAPS WITH DOUR EXPRESSIONS JOSTLE DISCONTENTEDLY. A CAR APPROACHES.

Worker 1   Here he comes . . . smoking that big fat cigar . . .

Worker 2   In his bloody flash Mercedes Benz . . .

Worker 1   You'd think he could afford better than that with all the overtime he did last week.

Worker 2   (SHOUTS) Oi! Careful where you park . . . nearly grazed my Porsche.

Worker 1   Look out — here's the gaffer.

Boss   Why aren't the men at work, Rushton?

Worker 1   We've come out.

Boss   I hope this doesn't mean you're going to start wearing women's clothes.

Worker 1	No, sir.
Boss	Good, 'cause I'm the only one round here who does that.
Worker 1	The face workers are out as well, sir.
Boss	Does this mean I'm not going to get my nose-job finished in time . . .?
Worker 2	(DOURLY) We're out in sympathy with our brother Joss Ackroyd . . . who the management has left on the scrapheap.
Boss	But that was his job . . . he was scrapheap attendant.
Worker 2	And another thing. Since our brother's unfair dismissal safety standards down t'pit have seriously deteriorated.
Worker 1	Aye, he was the best pit-prop we ever had.
Worker 2	Aye, especially with his flat head.
Boss	Listen . . . there's the hooter . . . now come on back to work.
Worker 1	We're not budging till the wrong has been righted.
Boss	I see.
Worker 1	Aye.
Worker 2	Aye.
Worker 1	Eee ba gum.
Worker 2	Ee 'up.

(DRAMATIC PAUSE)

CLOSING CREDITS. THEME TUNE OF BRASS BAND PLAYING HOVIS ADVERT MUSIC. THE END.

FAMOUS RICH PEOPLE (1)

Sir Kitchen Sinklair

The Computer King

Sir Kitchen was born in the small Cambridgeshire town of Impington, which came as a great shock to his parents who were both in Edinburgh at the time. He had a very normal childhood, except for the extremely abnormal bits of which there were many. His family were not rich, but they made up for it by having a lot of money and keeping it in the bank. As a result, they could afford to send Kitchen to the expensive Perse Public School — just a stone's throw from a lot of broken windows.

Sir Kitchen, whose real name was never known — after his grandfather Never Known Sinklair — loved Maths at school. He was fascinated by numbers. His favourite even numbers were 6,218 and 766. His favourite odd number was 'Shaddappa Your Face' by Joe Dolce.

As a boy he stunned his parents with his genius; as a girl he stunned them with something else altogether. It was the Sixties . . . the era of flower-power. Indeed, Sir Kitchen tried to design a car driven by dahlias but with little success.

Kitchen knew the computer was going to take off in a major way. If only he could think of a way of making it small, then he knew he could make it big. The micro-chip had just been invented. It was a sort of mini-computer which could do thousands of jobs at a time. It was the nearest thing to magic since Gordon Banks' save against Brazil in 1970.

Sir Kitchen realised that he could make computers extremely cheaply by only exploiting a small part of the micro-chip's capability. This way anyone could afford a pocket calculator, which told you in seconds how many pockets you have . . . a transistor radio you could strap to your wrist . . . a word-processor you could carry around in a suitcase . . . a computer you could fit on the end of a biro.

Kitchen became a millionaire within five years. He couldn't have done better if he'd had hotels on Mayfair and Park Lane and both the utilities. He was flavour of the month, way ahead of pistachio and chocolate. He was in such favour that at a mere 32 years old he was called to the Palace, where Terry Venables asked him to play in goal. By now he was Sir Kitchen — the richest man in his field . . . which was Selhurst Park.

At the time of writing this book, Sir Kitchen was working on a revolutionary new road vehicle, the C6 — a giant silver banana driven entirely by will-power.

THINGS TO DO WITH ALL YOUR MONEY NO. 103

Start a Price-cutting Trans-Atlantic Airline

This is definitely a good way of taking the strain off your wallet and seeing a few million quid literally disappear into thin air.

In the short term you become very popular with students, tourists and young people in general who desperately want to go to America but can't afford the regular fare.

In the long term you become very unpopular with the same students, tourists and young people who desperately want to get home but are stranded in America with worthless tickets for your airline which has unfortunately gone bust.

Buying a House

If you want a sound long-term investment for your money, why not buy a house? Everybody wants you to do it — the government, the building societies, your parents, your employers, most of all the person you're buying the house from.

Economically it makes perfect sense. After all, when you're living in rented accommodation, look at your outgoings:

● Rent

Whereas when you've bought your own home, you've only got this lot to consider:

● Mortgage repayments
● Rates
● Water rates
● Buildings insurance
● Ground rent
● Service charge
● Bills, repairs etc.

The first thing you need is a mortgage, which you get from your local building society.

Building societies are always quick to react to events. When interest rates go up, they quickly get together and announce a corresponding rise in the mortgage rate that very afternoon. And when interest rates go down, they quickly get together and announce that they'll be considering a reduction in the mortgage rate at the earliest opportunity, i.e. the first meeting of the Building Societies' Association on the second Tuesday of next month.

The only real drawback about getting involved in the property market is having to deal with estate agents.

Useful phrases that people use at dinner parties when discussing property . . .

- 'Jenny and Steve are looking further out . . .'
  (i.e. they've got better eyesight than most people)

- 'Geoffrey and Lisa are about to exchange . . .'
  (Geoffrey's about to become Lisa)

- 'Mike and Mandy have just completed . . .'
  (I bet Mike completed first)

Gambling

A common error people make about money is that you can save it. This is of course absolute nonsense. You cannot save money. All you can do is postpone the moment when you get rid of it.

And what better way of getting rid of it than by gambling? Though I never gamble myself, it's true that most people are partial to an occasional flutter. Do *you* gamble . . . ? I'm willing to bet that you do.

Gambling, as a way of spending money, is remarkably similar to flushing it down the lavatory, with the advantage that you don't have to go to lavatories which are often damp, fetid places redolent of shit, squalor and Nigel Rees (though it has to be said that a lot of bookmakers' shops are very similar).

Horse-racing

This is a system where the 'punter' or 'mug' hands over a certain amount of money to a 'bookmaker' or 'moneymaker' for the duration of a horse race. At the end of the race the bookmaker keeps the money.

Greyhound-racing

The principles of greyhound-racing are similar to those of horse-racing. Horses run because they have on their backs a stunted man, dressed in ridiculous clothes and a silly peaked cap, who hits them on the rump with a whip. Greyhounds, who have a slightly lower IQ than horses, run because they hope to catch a white nylon furry rabbit which streaks around the track on an electric rail.

Poker

Poker is surely one of the most entertaining ways of losing money in that it combines two of the most basic human needs: sitting around with your friends and lying to them.

Public Phone Boxes

A relatively new form of gambling involving smaller sums of money (10p, 20p, 50p). The idea of the game is that you put a coin in the slot and, if you win, you get to talk to someone on the phone. Unlike other slot machine games there are no 'hold' or 'nudge' buttons but nevertheless public telephones are very popular, possibly due to their unique atmosphere of stale urine and Chinese food.

★ LANDMARKS IN FINANCIAL HISTORY ★

The Wall Street Crash

Everybody with investments in the stock market — unit trusts, gilt-edged stocks, penny shares, gold bonds — will remember the Wall Street Crash of '29.

Unfortunately I've got none of these things so I can't remember it at all; in fact, I thought the phrase referred to some ghastly pop group who turn up occasionally on the Des O'Connor Show.

The Wall Street Shuffle

Not so much a landmark in financial history as a record by 10CC that reached No. 10 in the charts in 1974.

★ ★

Accountants

Accountants are traditionally regarded as rather boring.

This is sheer prejudice which exists partly because their work is not understood by the general public, partly because much of what they do is confidential and cannot be discussed with friends, and partly because they are in fact very dull people.

Accountants can be subdivided into Chartered Accountants, Certified Accountants, Cost Accountants and Turf Accountants.

Being a Certified Accountant does not mean that the accountant in question has been certified and committed to a lunatic asylum. If you suggest that to a Certified Accountant he is likely to get annoyed or, even more likely, to yawn, since he will doubtless have heard the remark many times before.

This is because there aren't many jokes to be made about accountants, except to point out that Certified Accountants are mad and that accountants themselves are boring.

Self-employed people employ accountants in order to reduce

their tax bills. For example, if you appear to have made a profit over the year of £1,000, and are consequently due to pay £200 in tax, any good accountant ought to be able to do enough work to reduce this to zero.

For this he will charge £250.

Accountants are traditionally wary individuals. There's the story of the seemingly rich man who hired a personal accountant for £30,000 a year to take care of all his problems.

'Where are you going to get the £30,000?' asked the sharp-witted accountant.

'That's your first problem,' he replied.

Starting Your Own Business . . .

As a way of getting rich, starting your business — which may involve years of hard work and determined struggle but which will hopefully lead one day to country estates, Rolls Royces and yachts in the South of France — is second only to being the son or daughter of someone who started his own business, in which case you still get the country estates, Rolls Royces and yachts but skip the hard work and determined struggle.

So how do you do it?

(1) Think of something that nobody's thought of before, such as . . . er . . . well, obviously if I told you you'd think of it before me, so don't think I'm going to fall for that one.

(2) Borrow a lot of money from bank manager/Daddy/any rich friends you may happen to have.

(3) Spend most of it on breakfast at the Savoy/lots of new clothes/skiing holidays/sex/anything else you've been promising yourself for ages.

(4) Use the rest to start up an incredibly successful business which makes you a legendary tycoon in the Richard Branson/Clive Sinclair mould.

(5) Hire lots of other people to do the work and retire to the South of France.

Easy, isn't it?

£££££££££££££££££££££££££

• Middlemen •

One of the reasons that everything seems to be so expensive in life is that in any transaction there are always half a dozen or so middlemen creaming off a fat percentage for doing very little indeed.

Take this book, for instance. We wrote it. You're reading it. If it was as simple as that it probably wouldn't cost more than 50p, and we'd both be happy (50p being rather less than you've paid for it and considerably more than we're ever likely to see at the end of the day).

Instead of which there are all sorts of shadowy figures — publishers, agents, editors — trying to get their grubby hands on the loot. It makes me sick. Publishers, in particular, are the very worst sort of parasite. They sit in their chintzy offices in Covent Garden digesting the lunch that they've bought themselves with the proceeds of our hard labour, sending back lovingly prepared manuscripts with curt letters beginning 'With regret . . .'

And the worst thing of all about these snotty-nosed Oxbridge English graduates is that if they don't like what you've written they just

I call this censorship! (There were actually some very good
bits on this page.)

All right — we give in!

· Middlemen ·

In any advanced consumer society you will find that as well as the people who produce the goods and the people who buy them, there are a number of so-called 'middlemen' who are involved in the business of distribution, marketing, designing and packaging.

These people play a vital, often unrecognised role in the creative process and indeed it would scarcely be possible to get by without them.

Many of them work long, arduous hours for little reward, and they certainly earn their 15% or whatever it is that they charge as a purely nominal fee or 'honorarium'.

In fact, let's hear it for the so-called middlemen — the whole   bunch of them.

— Money Arounc

A guide to other nations' money, to remind us that however weak the pound sterling is, at least it isn't called by a silly name like 'lek' or 'rouble'.

ALBANIA

Lek: Since there is nothing to buy in Albania and nothing to sell, it seems rather strange that they should have a currency at all. So the Lek is totally without worth or merit (see also *Leek*, national symbol of Wales).

ARGENTINA

Peso: The Spanish for 'weight', and this can be up to three days in an Argentinian bank.

AUSTRALIA

Dollar: One of the strongest currencies in the world. For 10 dollars you can buy a crate of Australian lager and half an hour with a typical good-time Sheila. If you're prepared to pay 100 dollars you can get one can of the lager and just 5 minutes with the Sheila.

AUSTRIA

Schilling: Very similar to the old British coin except that it's spelled wrong, due to the Austrian habit of putting in an unnecessary 'c'. This shows what a rappy bunh of unts they are.

BELGIUM/ LUXEMBOURG

Franc: Exactly the same currency as France, just so that neither of these places retains any sense of national identity or individuality, both of which are against the law in Belgium.

BRAZIL **Cruzeiro:** Brazil is the only country in Latin America to be named after a former Manchester United footballer. The cruzeiro is stronger than most South American currencies due to the successful export of coffee. In fact Brazil is famous mostly for its coffee and its late-night carnivals. The carnivals go on all night because nobody can get to sleep because of the coffee . . . and even if you could get to sleep you'd be constantly woken up by the bloody all-night carnivals.

FRANCE   **Franc:**   Named by knocking a letter off the end of the name of the country.

GERMANY   **Mark:**   Commonly known as the Deutsch Mark to distinguish it from other well known 'marks', e.g. Alfred and Karl, the ones you get in your underpants, and the ones that Portugal never get in the Eurovision Song Contest. Most Germans are very rich and can be seen lying on Greek and Spanish beaches reading books like *Teach Yourself Humour* and *100 Years of Invasion*.

GREECE   **Drachma:**   The famous Greek philosopher Socrates once oaid of money. 'κε katherl na prepl then lepi oute to krasioume tha parali sas plirosa arketa ti prepi na kanou.' And I think that's as true today as it was 2,400 years ago.

ICELAND   **Krona:**   The only nation in Europe still to use margarine as its currency.

INDIA   **Rupee:**   Not to be confused with a 'grupee', which is a girl who hangs around the dressing rooms of Indian rock stars; not that there are any Indian rock stars unless you count Ravi Shankar and George Harrison.

ITALY   **Lira:**   The smallest and most irritating thing about Italy apart from Fiat 600s, parmesan cheese and those tight poncey shoes worn by hairdressers. There are about 10,000 lire to the pound. You can have a decent meal with wine in Rome for a mere 4,000,000,000 lire. If you had a 1 lira coin for every hydrogen atom in the Pacific Ocean you'd have enough money to buy a double duvet cover from Marks & Spencers.

JAPAN **Yen:** One of the strongest currencies imaginable. So strong, in fact, that changing Yens into sterling is a form of ritualistic suicide like Hari Kiri or Kame Kazi or driving a second-hand Toyota.

MEXICO **Peso:** There's little to be said about the Mexican Peso except to quote this letter from a bank manager.

'Dear Mexico,
It has come to my attention that at close of business on Friday your account was in debit to the tune of £805,910,000,000.★ Despite promises to the contrary you continue to use the cheque encashment facility with insufficient funds to back it up. I gather that your only work at present is appearing in the background of cowboy movies. Until sufficient monies are introduced into your account I would ask you to refrain from cashing cheques and would request you to cut your Barclaycard in two returning one half to me.

Yours sincerely,
F. Blenkinsop

NETHERLANDS **Guilder:** Originally this was pronounced 'builder' until ventriloquy caught on in a big way in Holland.

SPAIN **Peseta:** There's nothing I can say about the peseta — or anything Spanish — now which couldn't be said just as well tomorrow.

★ See *The bank manager letters* for an explanation of this tune.

USA   **Dollar:**   On a good day the pound sterling is the same as a dollar . . . on a bad day the pound sterling is the same as a cent.

USSR   **Rouble:**   Russian currency runs on a completely different monetary standard to Western Europe so it's difficult to equate them accurately. Here is a rough guide.

Sterling	*Roubles*
1 Mars bar	= 50 Roubles
1 medium fresh orange	= 100 Roubles
1 girlie magazine	= 500 Roubles
1 pair Levi jeans	= 1,000 Roubles
1 team photo Manchester United FC	= 2,000 Roubles
1 old Beatles album	= 3,000 Roubles
1 British passport	= 250,000 Roubles, my pretty little sister, my *Das Kapital* and as many of those little wooden dolls which open up with other little wooden dolls inside as you want.
1 Nigel Rees paperback	= 3 Roubles (if you're lucky)
1 soiled condom	= 5 Nigel Rees paperbacks.

Monotony

Go 👉	Old Kent Road £60 **1**	Income Tax Pay £1,000 **2**	South of the River £10 **3**	✈ Luton Airport £1,000 **4**	Chance	Highbury £8 **5**	Just Jail Visiting **6**
Mayfair £400 **22**							Water Co. £150 **7**
Supertax £100 **21**							County Hall **8**
Port Stanley Airport £20,000,000 **20** ✈							Community Chest **9**
Community Chest **19**							Gatwick Airport £1,000 ✈
Oxford Street £300 **18**							Vine Street £200 **10**
Green Park £20 **17**							Docklands £0 **11**
👉 Go to Jail **16**	Electric Co. £150 **7**	Euston Road £6.50 **15**	Heathrow Airport £1,000 ✈	Fleet Street £220 **14**	Strand £220 **13**	Birmingham £2.50 **12**	National Parking Pay £50

1 Only London Street still to retain its original Monopoly value

2 Pay accountant £5,000 to celebrate

3 Lies outside London cabbies' 'Thirty-Yard Rule'

4 You have won 2nd prize in beauty competition: other players take this opportunity to draw attention to your physical defects, pimples, BO, etc.

5 Includes market value of current Arsenal squad

6 Visit to last anything between 2 and 30 years (see 16)

7 Not for sale until privatised

8 Price to be announced

9 Go to jail and try to stay there as long as possible to avoid paying rent

10 Where?

11 Rent £10,000 p.a., payable some time in the next century

12 ONO

13 So called because it's impossible to find a cab

14 Plus £30,000 in bribes to editors of national newspapers

15 Represents amount run up on taxi meter during typical quarter-mile stretch

16 Two years for each house illegally built, 8 years for each hotel

17 (a) Fine for allowing your dog to shit on the grass (b) Reward for anyone who manages to walk through the park without treading in one of the huge piles of dogshit

18 So called because it goes all the way to Marble Arch

19 Advance to Go — just when you thought you were going to land on Mayfair and Park Lane

20 So far

21 Annoying, eh?

22 Per hour, per variation, per prostitute

35

Bank Holidays

Ever since the Fall of Man in the Garden of Eden we have been cursed with anguish, grief and suffering. Because we failed, God has visited much pestilence upon us. Apart from the obvious ones . . . disease, hatred, war, poverty, jealousy and greed . . . all of which can be quite fun at the right time and in small doses . . . there are the subtler ones . . . those tiny irksome things which make life on this planet so unbearable: jazz, Yorkshiremen, computer games, loose paving stones that squirt water up your trousers when you step on them, the Bishop of Durham, German wine, German anything else, biros that don't work, art galleries, people who come up to you at parties and ask what star sign you are . . . and of course bank holidays.

Here are a few suggestions of things you can do to make bank holidays pass that much quicker:

- Take your family to the seaside and try to slip back home without them noticing.
- Rob a bank . . . and this is a particularly good time to do it since they're all on holiday.
- Walk around the streets wearing lilac pyjamas and tell the arresting officer you're looking for a flower bed.
- Bury the neighbour's dog in your garden.
- Kill the neighbour's dog first and *then* bury it in your garden.

- Go to a fancy dress party with a used Durex on the end of your nose and when somebody asks you what you've come as say 'F*** knows!'
- See how many times you can read the *Mirror* in 60 seconds.
- Strangle somebody close to you.

Personally, I have tried all these things, and can state with confidence that they add vitality and excitement to miserable wet bank holidays.

A lot of people think there's something wrong with my head, but I've looked at it very carefully and it seems to be exactly the same as all the other heads in my collection.

Robbing a Bank . . .

Compared with discovering an oil well or starting your own home computer business, robbing a bank is quite a complicated way of getting rich.

It involves considerable expertise, needs to be meticulously planned and contains a certain element of risk.

On the other hand it does have the advantage that you don't have to pay tax on earnings.

The first step is to choose a bank and decide when you're going to do it. You may need an entire weekend to tunnel through the foundations, but don't worry — Bank Holidays were invented specifically for this purpose.

Then all you have to do is recruit some fellow robbers from among your criminal friends, hire a getaway car and put the plan into operation.

Unfortunately, even if you're not caught, robbing a bank is punishable by having to live in South America with a repugnant bunch of cockney wide-boys with chunky jewellery, beer guts and peroxide wives.

£ £

Economics

Why is news about the British economy always bad?

This is one of the great mysteries of life, ranking alongside such questions as what happened to the people on board the *Marie Celeste*, why do London buses always travel in groups of three, and what does anybody see in Richard Stilgoe?

Take the pound's exchange rate against the dollar. This is always too high, too low, or too medium.

If it is too low, this is regarded as absolute proof of national decline . . . 'Pound worth less than dollar shock!' . . . 'Bank of England powerless!' . . . 'Government defends strategy!'

If, on the other hand, it rises a few cents, the CBI, TUC, MCC and any number of other shadowy bodies soon weigh in with the complaint that our exports are being priced out of foreign markets . . . essential to retain competitive edge . . . must be able to beat the Taiwanese . . . national decline imminent . . . England follow on in Test Match.

The same is true of oil. There was a time when all the experts predicted doom and gloom for Britain because we had no native oil resources . . . the very rock on which the ship of state will founder . . . no control over vital asset . . . constant drain on balance of payments etc.

All that changed when North Sea oil was discovered in the mid-60s. Was there dancing in the streets, national celebration, grown men weeping openly out of relief and exhilaration?

Yes, but only because England had won the World Cup.

So what can be done?

In think-tanks in Whitehall, laboratories in Cambridge and economics faculties the length and breadth of the country, small teams of people have been trying for years to construct a successful, all-embracing model of the British economy. The idea being that if you can only build a model of the economy you'll be able to find out what's going wrong. And if you can only establish what's going wrong you'll soon be able to put it right.

This is rather like saying that if you can only work out that you're 4–0 down with five minutes to go, the fact that you know you need 5 goals will make them that much easier to score.

One of the most difficult things to establish is exactly how money circulates within the economy.

Take the typical consumer who goes into Sainsbury's and goes out again with £10 worth of groceries.

The first question to ask is, why didn't he pay for them? This is certainly what the burly security man on the door will want to know.

But supposing he does pay up. At the end of the transaction Sainsbury's will be £10 better off, and the consumer £10 worse off. But it's not as simple as that. Sainsbury's will have had to buy these same groceries from manufacturers and wholesalers. And, then again, a fair amount of the profit goes to the government in tax.

Nor does it stop there. Sainsbury's have got their employees' wages to consider, and the rent and rates on the premises, and handling costs, bank interests etc.

In fact, it makes you wonder why it's worth running Sainsbury's at all: there can't be a lot of profit in it.

The answer, of course, is that they don't make their money out of groceries: they make it out of charging the absurd sum of 4½p for a plastic carrier bag.

★ LANDMARKS IN FINANCIAL HISTORY ★

The Tolpuddle Martyrs

The Tolpuddle Martyrs were punished in 1834 for forming a trade union, refusing to hold a postal ballot, not voting Conservative etc. Strictly speaking they weren't martyrs at all since they were only sent to Australia, though it could be argued that that amounts to much the same thing.

★ ★

British Currency

British Currency

Until 1971 Britain had a rather interesting though somewhat confusing currency in which 12 pence were worth 1 shilling and 20 shillings were worth £1.

Nowadays we have a modern, up-to-date, thrusting coinage in which £1 is worth practically nothing.

The idea of having a decimal currency was thought of in 1849 when the florin (2 shillings, or $\frac{1}{10}$ of a pound) was first minted. Decimal currency was finally brought in in 1971 — 122 years later.

Even then the idea of dividing the pound into such tidy divisions as $\frac{1}{100}$ths seemed very un-English, so half-pennies were brought in as well to retain a bit of confusion for idiots and foreigners.

Unfortunately time and inflation has done away with them (half-pennies, that is, not idiots and foreigners).

Today British currency is a mixture of coins (copper and silver) and bank notes. Bank notes in England are issued exclusively in the Bank of England. There are also three banks in Scotland issuing notes, which are put into circulation mainly to start arguments in pubs around King's Cross.

Paper Money

All British bank notes are spoiled by having endless inky squiggles scribbled all over them by bored Bank of England staff. Other distinguishing features include old and remarkably unlife-like photographs of the Queen (whose name they can never remember, as they always call her Queen Er . . .) and an autograph by the chief cashier whose handwriting is completely illegible. Presumably he's a former doctor.

By folding notes above the Queen's chin, the line of her jaw and her neck form the famous pub-joke phenomenon known as the Queen's bum. There is a thin line of metal down the middle of most bank notes, revealed when the note is held up to the light. This is a device to help forgers not to get real ones muddled up with their own.

The famous old £1 note, soon to be withdrawn from circulation — and no wonder. The Queen looks particularly out of sorts in this photograph, with lollipops stuck to her sleeves and a frumpy, embarrassed look on her face — presumably due to the large branches of apple blossom growing out of her hair. She is sitting on a table next to an old 'What-the-butler-saw' machine and a Toblerone. On the wall to her right is a large ancient Egyptian dartboard.

The £5 note, and another very dubious likeness of the Queen. In this one she obviously hasn't shaved for a few days and has adopted a fashionable man's hairstyle. For some reason she's carrying some rope over her right shoulder — perhaps she uses it to help intruders break into her bedroom.

On her chest she is wearing the plastic sheriff's badge that she won in a Christmas cracker aged eight.

One of the Queen's favourite hobbies is horse-racing, and to her right is a large painting of the pile-up at Beecher's Brook in the 1849 Grand National.

The £10 note. In this photo the Queen cleverly covers up her Sony Walkman with a frilly scarf, but you can still see the wire dangling down the front.

For no apparent reason she is holding a Cycling Proficiency test certificate.

To her right is a picture of a room in which some official-looking people are counting money and others are lying around waiting, looking bored or starving to death. Obviously a post office.

The £20 note. In this picture, bizarrely, the Queen looks exactly like the well-known playwright William Shakespeare, who in turn looks somewhat stoned and seems to be thumping himself in the mouth.

Shakespeare lived rough, played rough and sometimes even wore a ruff — but not in this picture. He obviously got fed up with people making jokes about it. Similarly the tights.

To the Queen's right is a representation of a scene from one of Shakespeare's most famous plays, *Hamlet*. Hamlet is doing his famous 'To be or not to be' monologue when Juliet appears on the balcony and says 'Shit, I'm in the wrong theatre.'

The £50 note. A sad picture of the Queen, inasmuch as a new conditioner recommended to her by her official hairdresser has caused her to go completely bald, and she has felt obliged to pour an enormous quantity of chocolate mousse over her head to cover it up.

She obviously intends to get her own back as she has in her hand a sharp pair of compasses.

To the right of her hand is the secret plan for a new space ship, above which is a picture of St Paul's Cathedral surrounded by dolls' houses and a miniature boating lake.

Slang Words for Money

Bread   This word has been used for years as a euphemism for money, mainly by bakers who correctly observed that if they didn't make any bread they wouldn't make any money . . . if you see what I mean.

Dough   An old baking expression. Bakers realised that before they made any bread — or any bread — they'd have to have some dough. Hence: dough, meaning dough.

Motza   Yiddish slang for money. It is also the Hebrew word for bread.

Readies   Cash. From the old bakery expression 'Are those loaves ready yet, Mr Baker?'

Loot   Hindi word for 'plunder' . . . or goods stolen . . . usually from a bakery.

Wonga   African word for 'gym shoe'. Sometimes used to mean 'bread' by people who haven't bothered to revise their African vocabulary.

Rhino   Old-fashioned word for money. Vaguely connected with the horned pachyderm and not in any way connected with bread or bakers, except that a baker once got gored by a rhino in Milton Keynes. It never made the news, of course . . . but had the baker gored the rhino, well . . .

Ackas   (a) Corruption of 'hackers', i.e. knives used to cut rough bread (see *bread, dough, motza, readies, wonga, rhino* etc.). (b) Industrial conciliation body which decides which side in a dispute gets the bread (i.e. management).

Shekels   Hebrew for small coins . . . shaped like baps and made from dough.

Mazuma   Mexican bread God.

★ LANDMARKS IN FINANCIAL HISTORY ★

The Repeal of the Corn Laws

Until 1846 foreign corn was subject to heavy import duties. The repeal of the Corn Laws was regarded at the time as a great success, but it did lead eventually to dreadful disasters — Sacha Distel, Rolf Harris, Paul Hogan, the Made Silly series etc.

★ ★

The Stock Exchange

The motto of the Stock Exchange is 'Dictum Meum Pactum' or 'My premium is my bond'.

Originally the Stock Exchange was a café in the city where the service was so bad that customers amused themselves while waiting for attention by buying stocks and shares, blowing South Sea bubbles and speculating in coffee futures (e.g. 'Do you think that expresso is ever going to arrive?').

Members of the Stock Exchange have two main aims in life:

(1) To make a lot of money
(2) To think up silly names for each other, for example:

Brokers
Brokers are so called because portions of a company's equity are divided up and sold off to people investing their money on the advice of stockbrokers. Quite often this money is lost and the people go broke.

Jobbers
Under sweeping reforms soon to be introduced to the Stock Exchange the functions of jobbers and brokers are to be combined. The result will be known as a 'joker'.

Bulls and Bears
Bulls buy shares when they think the price is going to go up, Bears when they think it will go down. On the face of it the Bulls seem to have got the better of the deal. The word Bull

derives from the garbage people come out with when they are trying to talk up the value of the share they have just bought (see under *Bullshit*).

Bullshit
See under *Bulls*.

Stags
People who buy new issues of shares and sell them immediately, usually at a great profit, are known as stags, because like the animals they go round in herds, are very nervous and have large horns growing out of their heads.

£ £ **WAYS OF GETTING RICH NO. 583** £ £

Writing a Pop Classic . . .

One of the very best ways of making your fortune is to write a song that sells millions of copies and gets played on the radio for years to come in 'oldies' shows.

For example if you were to dash off any old lyrics like 'Yesterday/All my troubles seemed so far away/Now it looks as though they're here to stay/Oh I believe in yesterday' and get them played constantly on the radio the money would come rolling in.

But of course you'd need it to pay for the crippling law suit with Paul McCartney.

£££££££££££££££

Putting It in a Numbered Swiss Bank Account

This is a popular ruse, particularly if you came by your money in ways you would rather not disclose.

People always refer to Swiss bank accounts as being 'numbered', though why this is the case is a mystery, since all bank accounts are numbered. The number of mine, for instance, is 21027713.

Interestingly enough, although the only person who can take money out of a bank account is the person in whose name the account is held, more or less anyone can put money into it. All you need is one of those little pink slips of paper, the number of the account and the name (Peter Fincham).

How to Manage Your

'A bank manager is a person who will lend you an umbrella on a sunny day then take it off you when it starts raining.'
Ambrose Bierce

There are two sorts of bank manager:

(1) Nice ones
(2) Your own.

A lot of people think that bank managers are people who have failed in life . . . people who bear a grudge against their fellow men . . . people who are neurotic about the size of their genitalia . . . dull, grey people with dull, grey minds and dull, grey clothes.

This may or may not be true but it's not worth mentioning to your bank manager except as a last resort.

Remember that nearly 90% of bank managers are human too. They have all the pressures, worries and problems that other people have . . . and it bloody well serves them right.

It's very easy to make fun of bank managers, which is presumably why most people do it.

But when corresponding with your bank manager, try to remain polite, courteous and if necessary just sycophantic. Then if this doesn't work turn nasty. The letters which follow are a typical example of one unfortunate man's monthly correspondence with his bank manager.

Bank Manager

4/2/86

Dear Mr Bell,

It has come to our attention that at close of business on Friday your account was in debit to the tune of £500. Please refrain from using the cheque encashment facility until sufficient monies are introduced into this account.

Yours sincerely,
G. P. Lane

This is a typically dull bank manager letter . . . leaden and prosaic. Notice the 'Dear Mr Bell'. The 'dear' here is not a sign of affection but 'dear' in its financial sense meaning 'expensive, costly'. He uses 'our' instead of 'my' in order to pass on responsibility for making your life a misery to his faceless colleagues . . . so that when you eventually decide to get your revenge by chucking a petrol bomb through his window you might not choose him as your victim. Don't be put off by this tactic.

'Close of business' means 3.30 p.m., i.e. round about the middle of lunch. 'In debit' is included because 'debit' is the only word of Latin that most bank managers know.

'To the tune of £500 . . .' Pure banking jibberish. There is no tune of £500 . . . so far as I know there isn't even a song lyric of that name.

'Cheque encashment facility' and 'monies' — more bank-managerese. 'Monies' is a particular favourite, meaning —

surprisingly — money. I've no idea why bank managers use this expression and can only imagine that it must have been a misprint in *Teach Yourself Banking* and that all managers have stuck to it. However, this is for the most part a standard bank manager's letter.

Here is the standard reply.

231 Acacia Ave,
Grimedale-by-the-Sea

6/2/86

Dear Mr Lane,

Thank you for your kind and informative letter. But for your communication I would not have noticed that I had spent more than I had in my account. How remiss of me. I shall endeavour to rectify this situation forthwith. I am owed monies well in excess of £500 and will not draw on the account again until said monies are introduced into the account.

Many thanks again for the information.

Yours,
S. Bell

There are two important things about a standard reply of this sort: (1) none of it is remotely true (2) it is a parody as cruel as possible of the silly prose style of the original. The bank manager will not become aware of either of these things until much later in the correspondence.

Barclloyd's Bank,
High Street,
Grimedale-by-the-Sea

7/2/86

Dear Mr Bell,

  Thank you for your letter. I am pleased you are owed monies and that you will not be drawing on the account until these are paid in. However, since last Friday your overdraft has increased from £500 to £3,789.63p. No monies have yet been introduced. If the situation continues the bank will be forced to get the money from you by means of the law.

 Yours sincerely,
 G. P. Lane

There is only one way to deal with letters of this sort — ignore them. Write back immediately with lie No. 56.

The Gardens,
Kensington High Street,
London W8

12/2/86

Dear Mr Lane,

  Excuse the delay — your letter took some time reaching me. You'll be delighted to know that I finally tracked down the person who was fraudulently using my Barclaycard and he is now in police custody. It will be some months before the case comes to court but in the meantime I will attempt to bring the account into a non-debit situation.

 Yours relieved,
 S. Bell

A good tactic. Incredible to a normal human being but just about believable to a bank manager. The inclusion of a phrase like 'non-debit situation' is particularly clever. It may well be one that the bank manager hadn't thought of himself, and therefore he'll probably be using it throughout lunch. Nevertheless, the bank manager is starting to become sceptical about your promises. He starts examining your cheques to see what you're spending your money on.

> *Barclloyd's Bank,*
> *High Street,*
> *Grimedale-by-the-Sea*

17/2/86

Dear Mr Bell,
> *I was sorry to hear that your father had died again and that the funeral costs were even higher than last time. I notice another excessive payment of alimony to your former wife Victoria Wines. I would be grateful if you could cut your cheque card in two and send one of the pieces to me, which to avoid further damage I will have encased in lead and buried in the Pacific Ocean. You will be getting no more cheque books until monies have been introduced to your account to the tune of £11,984.00.*

> *Yours,*
> *G. P. Lane*

A heavy letter. And another non-existent tune! It's time to go for a bit of sympathy.

Platform 5,
King's Cross Station,
London N1

23/2/86

Dear Mr Lane,

      Thank you for your kind letter. And thank you for the patience and understanding your bank has shown to me throughout this year which has been a difficult time for me both personally and emotionally. I am glad I stayed with the Bank of Toytown and didn't get seduced by the other banks with their promises of free biros and imitation-leather cheque book covers.

    Yes, my father has died again. He is not a well man. You will be pleased to know that my drug rehabilitation programme is coming along nicely, and I have made some bona fide attempts to curb my expenditure, for instance by moving from my penthouse flat in Kensington to Platform 5 at King's Cross Station. This has saved me a lot of money but my health is suffering. I am not sleeping well because of the noise of the diesel engines and the nauseating smell of British Rail breakfasts and people from Newcastle.

    If you would just advance me another loan I will hire a gun and send my brains on a short journey by air. I don't blame you, Mr Lane . . . I wish I knew your Christian name, I feel sure you must have one . . . I blame the system.

Yours in extremis,
Simon

This sort of letter just might work . . . the trouble is that bank managers forget that people are human and not just figures in red or black.

Barclloyd's Bank,
High Street,
Grimedale-by-the-Sea

27/2/86

Dear Mr Bell,
　　　　I note your comments. I strongly advise you against committing suicide as this would have most unfortunate consequences. The bank would be left with your debit of £11,984.00 and no way of getting it back. May I suggest that you earn more money and spend less. I think this would be an admirable solution to your problem. I think you'll agree that you certainly do have a problem.

Yours sincerely,
G. P. Lane

Pragmatic shit. There's only one thing for it. Get heavy.

'Ocean Breeze',
c/o Royal Yacht Club,
Montserrat

15/3/86

Dear Mr Lane,
　　　　On the contrary, I think you *have the problem . . . I have over 11 grand of your money which you're not going to get back! I hope this won't affect your future with the bank.*

Yours,
S. Bell

If this doesn't work, try lobbing a petrol bomb through his window as mentioned earlier.

Credit Cards

'If money talks, credit cards are a convenient way of paying for items you can't really afford.'

Failed advertising copywriter

Credit cards have revolutionised the way we pay for goods and services. In the past, if we went to a shop and found something we wanted, we took money out of our wallet and paid for the item, receiving back change if necessary.

This was clearly most inconvenient, and has largely been replaced by the use of credit cards.

Instead of handing in cash, the card is handed to the shop assistant. The assistant then checks to see that the card is not listed as stolen, and — if the sum being paid is over a set limit — telephones the credit card company to clear the transaction.

The assistant then fills in a form (in triplicate) setting out the details of the transaction. Next the card and forms are inserted in a special machine which never works quite as smoothly as the person who designed it obviously thought it would.

The assistant then gets the customer (if he is still there) to sign the forms, gives him one copy and the card back and hey presto! the deal is done.

Of course there are other advantages to credit cards. Cash can be very easily stolen and used by a thief . . . whereas credit cards can be very easily stolen and used by a thief.

And the great thing about credit cards is that they keep a check on your spending by imposing an upper limit on your monthly transactions.

If you go over your limit the credit card company writes to you — just as a bank manager does if you overdraw your account. The difference is that whereas your bank manager writes to you in person (his secretary), with the credit card company it is always a computer speaking, and it's surprisingly difficult to take a computer seriously.

If you consistently exceed your limit, the company's demands get ever more fearsome, first demanding money by return of post, then that you return the card, and finally — as a last resort — suggesting that your credit limit is increased.

THINGS TO DO WITH ALL YOUR MONEY NO. 238

Supporting Struggling Writers and Artists

This sort of thing was very popular at the time of the Medicis and the Italian Renaissance but has rather dwindled since.

This is a shame. Writers are often considered a lazy, disreputable lot who don't have proper jobs and deserve all they get . . . which isn't much.

But many of them are actually sensitive and well-intentioned souls, struggling to earn a crust in a harsh, often unsympathetic world.

And have you seen the price of crusts nowadays?

Elmer Prescott

The King of Rock

Elmer Prescott was born Elmer Prescott and decided to change his name because he thought it sounded funny. So he changed it to Ivor Tinydick, realised his mistake and changed it back.

At the age of 16, Elmer dropped out of his Mississippi high school and became a full-time bum. His brothers were a right pair of tits, so they got together and posed for girlie magazines.

Then he started truck-driving for $2 a week. One day, a fellow driver of his lent him a guitar. Elmer never looked back. An old negro blues singer taught him four chords: C, D, G and that fiddly one where you have to put three of your fingers in an E shape, one finger flat over the top two strings and cock your thumb over the other side of the fret board . . . you know the one . . . yes, that's it.

Elmer began to sing around bars and college campuses. He was to revolutionise popular music by one simple fact — here was a white kid who could sing like a black kid. It had its drawbacks, of course. One night he got beaten up by a colour-blind member of the Klu-Klux-Klan.

He shot to fame and became a huge international star.

With stardom came money . . . from records, books, TV appearances, advertising and the $2 a week still coming in from the truck-driving. From now on he would want for nothing. As a result he started eating and drinking too much. He experimented with drugs and soon became an overweight physical wreck.

His personal life was in tatters. His second wife left him when she found out about the first. His first wife left him when she found out he'd been lying about the truck driving job by saying that it only paid $1 a week.

Scores of women came forward to say that he was the father of their children. Scores of men came forward to say that he was the mother of their children. The dream was turning into a nightmare. He was becoming more and more dependent on drugs. Uppers to get him up, downers to get him down, and when he was only half-way up he was neither up nor down.

He had all the money in the world, but he was slowly coming to realise that there's one thing — happiness — that you simply can't buy with money . . . though you can charge it up to your American Express card.

He killed himself with an overdose of hamburgers in 1977, and was buried with stately pomp which would befit a king. Forty-five of his close friends carried the coffin.

★ LANDMARKS IN FINANCIAL HISTORY ★

The South Sea Bubble

If there's one thing that every schoolboy knows all about, it's the South Sea Bubble of 1720. So if you happen to run into a schoolboy, ask him all about it.

Communism v. Capitalism

The world is split into two opposing camps, the capitalists and the communists.*

In the capitalist bit, the rich get richer and the poor complain a lot about their little — or a little about their lot — but in fact tend to get a little less poor as the years go by.

Whereas in the communist bit everybody is poor, except the people who join the Party and get rich.

So there we are. You can choose between the two . . . so long as you start off in the capitalist bit. If you start off in the communist bit — which was originally designed to free everybody from the tyranny of capitalism — you're free to do more or less anything except opt for the capitalist bit, or buy Western pop records, or stand in Red Square and say that in your opinion, all things considered, you think that Comrade Gorbachev is a tiny bit off his rocker.

Whereas if you start off in the capitalist bit you're perfectly free to move over to the communist bit — though they're liable to wonder what on earth you're up to and clamp you in jail for being a spy. This is because, in the eyes of the Russians, all Westerners are agents of imperialist reactionary capitalism, or capitalist reactionary imperialism, or something like that.

That's the wonderful thing about the Russians. Under

* Plus the Third World. If you've ever been to the Third World you'll realise why it came third. It is made up of areas of grinding poverty (not to be confused with 'dire poverty' or 'abject poverty' — see *Famous Rich People No. 2: Sheila Conwoman*), whose populations have lived in grinding poverty for hundreds of years and are likely to remain in similar grinding poverty for the foreseeable future. These are called 'developing countries'.

communism, you see, the capitalist class is removed, and the State soon withers away to a mere token presence of a million or so secret policemen, party committees, lunatic asylums for dissidents etc.

This is because the communists have got beyond the silly idea that the most important thing in life is to have money. The typical comrade in Moscow is well aware that the spirit of brotherly collectivism is far more rewarding than the materialist decadence of the West, represented by fast cars, night clubs and free speech. Nevertheless he'd like to pop over to the West just to check.

For many years experts, left-wing thinkers and other weirdos have predicted a period of crisis in capitalism followed by its inevitable and long overdue collapse. This sort of political crystal-ball gazing is very popular, so much so that those who practise it have made a great deal of money from their predictions, most of which they've wisely invested in American Long-Term Recovery Bonds.

Similarly, many people have felt over the years that the day must inevitably come when the down-trodden proletariat of the Eastern Bloc will rise up and demand to know who trod on them in the first place and why didn't they watch where they were going.

But like so many apocalyptic visions, this has yet to be proved right. The world trundles on much as before, with occasional East-West tensions but generally speaking a certain amount of peace and goodwill on both sides. Nobody really listens to the Harbingers of Doom any more — in fact their last couple of records have hardly made the charts.

So what of the future? For many years the West, and America in particular, was obsessed with the 'domino theory'

Made Really Very Simple

A Feature Article by Professor J. K. Brockstein

of world domination by the communists. This held sway until it was revealed that the Russians don't actually play dominoes, though they're pretty good at chess.

In the 1950s America, held in the grip of a 'reds under the bed' communist-infiltration panic, embarked on a national witch-hunt, but didn't manage to find any witches either.

In fact the Americans seem to have got it wrong from start to finish. This is the trouble with a society in which the money ethic rules supreme. Other values just disappear. Family loyalties, notions of right or wrong all become distorted in the eyes of the person whose only interest in life is money. Surely there is a better way.

CASHPOINTS

Your Money Problems Answered by Ann Expert . . .

Dear Ann,

       I am an unmarried mother. I live on the 27th floor of an inner-city tower block. I have three children all under five (or possibly the other way round). My rent and rates are paid by the DHSS and I receive £42 per fortnight to feed, clothe and otherwise look after me and my family.

Have you any tips as to how I can manage?

Frantic, Hackney.

Ann Expert writes: Money is obviously tight so you must be careful. I would recommend investing in government stocks, gilt-edged securities or possibly a unit trust, especially one with a Japanese or American bias. Otherwise look out for new issues such as British Airways, BT etc.

Dear Ann,

Can you settle an argument? I say there is no obligation to give a tip to a taxi driver. My friend, who happens to be a cab driver himself, says there is. Who is right?

Minnie, Cambridgeshire.

Ann Expert writes: I always give a tip to a cabbie. Since the disappearance of the old sixpence I generally give a shilling (5p). I don't think it is obligatory; in fact I usually find that the taxi driver is pathetically grateful to receive such a sum. Invariably I hear loud words of thanks, unfortunately in incomprehensible argot, being shouted after me as I make my way from the cab.

Dear Ann,

Both my parents died recently, leaving me as sole executor to look after their estate (a Volvo). I am still very upset by their deaths and I am finding it very hard to cope with all the practical problems and difficulties of sorting everything out. Can you advise?

B. Reaved, Kidderminster.

Ann Expert writes: A death in the family is always upsetting, especially when it happens to a relative. I do hope that you are finding support and consolation from those nearest and dearest to you: the surviving members of your family,

---

friends, and possibly your priest or minister. At a time like this you need help and understanding to enable you to come to terms with your grief. Still, you didn't write to me for that. You want to know how to deal with the stiffies' money, preferably to your own advantage. Frankly, I don't think that the complicated legal and financial problems created by a death in the family can be dealt with adequately in a problem page of this sort. I suggest you get proper advice by writing to 'Your Legal Problems Answered By a Lawyer'.

Dear Annie,

      I am desperately short of money. Can you lend me some?

    Pauper, the Embankment.

Ann Expert writes: *Piss off, will you? I am trying to run an advice column. I wouldn't send you any money if you were my own father.*

Dear Annie,

      For Christ's sake, I *am* your own father! Surely you can help me?

    Pauper, No Fixed Abode.

Ann Expert writes: *My own father! You should have said. Here's 25p for a cup of tea. It's more than I'd give a cab driver, you know.*

★ LANDMARKS IN FINANCIAL HISTORY ★

Devaluation of the Pound

Nobody could accuse Harold Wilson of inconsistency — for years he had been consistently saying that he wouldn't devalue the pound.

So in 1967 he did.

The devaluation of the pound is chiefly remembered for Harold Wilson's remark in which he said that it wouldn't make any difference to the 'pound in your pocket', i.e. it'll still look the same, feel the same and weigh the same — it'll just be worth less. (Or indeed worthless, as it's since become.)

★ ★

£ £ **WAYS OF GETTING RICH NO. 169** £ £

Get friendly with someone high up in Johnson Matthey bankers . . .

(Probably too late now.)

£££££££££££££££££

72

Children's Corner

The Story of Robin Hood

Robin Hood was a well-meaning chap, and thought that if he robbed from the rich and gave to the poor, the poor would be a lot happier and the rich wouldn't really notice the difference.

As a result, he was often called the father of Income Tax, though he denied this, saying that he'd only met the unmarried mother in question once at a party and nothing improper had taken place.

All were agreed, however, that Income Tax was a bastard of an invention, and it's a shame Robin didn't manage to patent the idea, since if he had he'd have become very rich indeed and could have robbed himself instead of mugging all those innocent sheriffs, government officials and rich barons.

Robin hung around in Sherwood Forest with his Merry Men and his live-in (or live-out, since they didn't have proper accommodation) girlfriend Marian in a sort of workers' cooperative or squat. In those days most people without money or property could be found in a squat — well, let's face it, the flush toilet simply hadn't been invented — and Robin was no exception.

Times were hard. Robin and the band divided their time

between hunting deer, practising archery and trying to get a record contract. How were they to know that it was to be 600 years before their theme tune 'Robin Hood, Robin Hood/ Riding through the glen' was to be a hit?

Little John even considered becoming a contortionist — just to make ends meet.

But Robin spent much of his time worrying about the poor. He suffered from a bad case of something that's never been conducive to making a lot of money: altruism.

Altruism is a noble quality when encountered in others, but well worth avoiding yourself. It is partly derived from a sense of guilt, and tends to afflict people who, like Robin, are young, good-looking, popular with the lads and have got really pretty girlfriends.

Friar Tuck, on the other hand, wasn't in the least bit altruistic — possibly because he was short, fat, unattractive to women and with a silly-looking bald patch. So far as he was concerned the poor could go and stuff themselves, which in fact was what Friar Tuck spent most of his time doing.

The villain of the piece was the Sheriff of Nottingham. He was an incredibly nasty, evil-minded piece of work, and had a very highly-developed sense of his own importance. He was so vain that he used to parade through the streets of Nottingham waving to the crowds from a horse-drawn carriage and trying to pass himself off as royalty.

People often mistook him for Torvill and Dean.

Time passed. Robin grew old, Maid Marian grew old. Will Scarlet grew old, Little John grew old. Friar Tuck grew young, but being a mean-minded little git he didn't pass this trick on to the others.

Eventually, after a lifetime's do-gooding, Robin lay on his

death bed, replete in the knowledge that he had taken an awful lot of money from the greedy, hard-drinking, lazy rich and given it to the needy, well-deserving poor (the poor had actually just used it to become lazy and hard-drinking like the rich, but they didn't tell Robin that so as to spare his feelings).

As the happy throng of Merry Men gathered round Robin's death bed, he had just one request: 'Wherever this arrow lands, bury me there.'

Gathering up his final reserves of strength, he took up his trusty bow, aimed as high as he could, and with his dying breath let go of the arrow.

So they buried him in the ceiling.

Money and How to Hang On to It

in Social Situations

In the Pub

As every schoolboy knows, it is the common law of England that drinks in pubs are bought in rounds. (And also that schoolboys are not allowed in pubs, but let that pass . . .) This is as much a part of the traditional British way of life as cricket on the village green, dog turds on the pavement, and Terry Wogan on the television.

The committed cheapskate (i.e. you, since you are reading this chapter) is very anxious never to buy the first round. Why?

This is because first rule of pubs (**Anderson's Law**, or the **Law of Diminishing Returns to the Bar**) states that: 'A drinker who starts with a pint of bitter sometimes follows it with a half, but if you start on halves you usually stay there.'

Or as Confucius put it: 'He who begins with a gin and tonic can continue with just a tonic, but it's a brave man who buys himself a Coca-Cola and later demands a double brandy. And by the way, mine's a large Grouse.'

What are the correct ways to behave for the committed cheapskate?

(1) Always hold the door open for your companion(s). This is not only polite, it means they get to the bar first.

(2) Never be provocative. Never say 'What are you having?' as this might provoke someone into replying.

(3) If notwithstanding (2) you say 'What are you having?' and your companion replies, 'No, let me' – let him.

(4) On arriving at the pub sit down at an empty table, saying you need to grab it for your group. (This is difficult in a full pub where you will have to eject the people already in occupation and manifestly ridiculous in a completely empty pub. But, remember, there is a cash saving to be made.)

(5) If desperate, go for the £50 Note Ploy. Cunningly you offer everyone a drink, and painstakingly take the various orders. Then, clapping hand to forehead for full effect, announce that you've only got a £50 note on you . . . impossibility of expecting change . . . crowded bar . . . etc., until somebody has to take over paying for the round instead of you. This trick is a particularly good one to pull as it clears you of the first round, *and all subsequent rounds*. It is also quite believable as tight bastards like you do get rich enough to have £50 notes on them as a matter of course. You cannot do this trick on the same people too often, though, as they will start bringing change of £50 (in which case you will have to actually have a £50 note for inspection). Also you cannot try the trick at all in the bar of a nightclub, most theatres, central London hotels, and other places where three drinks cost more than £50 anyway.

Once you have avoided the first round you can relax and since the stakes get lower on the next rounds you can use less subtle methods. Of which the elaborate Bavarian body-slapping dance to the tune of 'Where's my wallet, oh I must have left it in my other jacket' is best known.

Going to the lavatory when glasses seem to be getting empty is one way out.

The window is another way out (of the lavatory).

Or try saying you are off to feed the meter you left your car on. Best not tried at night, or if you all arrived in a taxi.

Otherwise, the elegant touch is to borrow the coins off the companions you are too stingey to buy drinks for.

By the way, the second rule of pubs (**Perkins' Law**) states that: 'When a group of intelligent, enlightened young people sit around in a pub discussing the various injustices in the world with particular reference to women in our society . . . it's still the men who end up buying the bloody drinks.'

In the Restaurant

Hanging on to your money at the end of a large meal involving a group of people is trickier, but well worth the effort since there are larger stakes involved.

Try leaving the meal early.

Brock's Law states that: 'The person who leaves the meal early conveniently forgets about the little things like cover charge, VAT, service and the vegetables.'

The person who does this and says 'I think a fiver should just about cover what I've had' will almost certainly get a bargain. He may also get a bit of stick from his friends when the bill eventually works out at £22.50 per head.

Assuming you're still there at the end of the meal, there are various ways of minimising the impact on your bank account.

(1) **'In Fairness to Hugo'**   Hugo is a vegetarian suffering from a digestive disorder and has only had the tomato soup and bread roll . . . which he didn't finish anyway. When the bill arrives you say in a loud voice 'In fairness to Hugo, I

think it's only right that we itemise the bill.'

Of course this is only a good idea if you yourself have had less than the average. If you're the person who ordered the lobster thermidor, the most expensive starter, then finished off two large brandies and dipped freely into the cigar box, stick to the time-honoured 'Let's split this right down the middle, shall we?' line.

(2) Grab the bill When the bill arrives a lot of people treat it as if it's tainted with some infectious disease. This is a mistake. Far better to say 'Now — let's have a look at this', grab the bill and make sure nobody else sees it.

Then, get in a muddle. Count up the number of people around the table. Adopt a look of studied concentration. Say 'Right — £13, everyone.' Let some money roll in, then study the bill again and say 'Actually, it's £9.50. No, I tell a lie — £11.' (NB Don't overdo this or somebody else may volunteer to do the arithmetic.)

In the ensuing confusion, the fact that you yourself only contributed £4 will hopefully go unnoticed.

(3) Blindfold the waiter If all else fails, call the waiter over and say 'Look — we can't decide who's going to pick up the bill. So what we want to do is blindfold you, spin you around, and then the person you point to has to pay. What do you think?'

Unless he's a particularly suspicious sort of character the waiter ought to agree to this agreeable plan.

By the time he realises what's going on, you and your friends have made your escape and be well on your way home, not having parted with a single penny.

It only remains cheap, of course, if you can get legal aid for the subsequent trial.

Tax

Income Tax was invented by William Pitt to pay for the Napoleonic Wars.

Nearly 200 years later it is still with us — making the Napoleonic Wars the most expensive in history.

A great deal of time and effort is spent in seeking ways of getting out of paying tax.

It is important to remember that *tax avoidance* is legal, honest, decent, respectable, praiseworthy, charming, acceptable and highly regarded the length and breadth of the land.

Whereas *tax evasion* is criminal, loathsome, vile, unjust, unfair, unacceptable, and despised by all right thinking men and women.

Or is it the other way round?

Various taxes and how to avoid (or evade) paying them . . .

Corporation Tax: This is easy. Simply avoid becoming a corporation.

Income Tax: This is a tricky one, and your best bet is probably to live abroad, though if you stay abroad long enough you'll end up having to pay tax in the country you've gone to unless you leave there quickly as well.

The recent popularity of Round-the-World yacht races owes much to this state of affairs (see also *Around The World in 80 Days* by Jules Pay-As-You-Vernes).

If you are going to settle in another country permanently it is as well to choose one whose tax rates are lower than the UK (i.e. avoid Sweden, though you probably would anyway).

Window Tax: This is best avoided by living after 1851, when it was abolished.

Value Added Tax: To most people VAT is simply one of five or six extra amounts you hadn't bargained for when the bill comes to you at the end of a meal in a restaurant.

Stamp Duty: To most people, Stamp Duty is simply one of 50 or 60 extra amounts you hadn't bargained for when the solicitor's bill comes to you after you've bought a house.

Death Duties: A tax on the property passing to next-of-kin. This was abolished some time ago as people were deliberately keeping other people alive, probably to avoid paying this tax (or possibly because they were doctors).

Death Duties have been replaced by **Capital Transfer Tax,** which means that people who inherit stately homes still have to sell a few bits of our British national heritage (usually Italian paintings) to pay for the roof, until the lions and funfair start paying for themselves.

Capital Gains Tax: This is a very clever tax which means that if you buy something today and sell it in a few years' time for a higher sum you have to pay tax on your gain.

It is described as clever because the government brought it in just before introducing galloping inflation, which meant that everyone found they were making 'gains' as the value of the pound went down.

Capital Gains Tax can be avoided by only buying things which are unlikely to increase in value such as Austin Allegros, Ra-Ra skirts, Bay City Rollers LPs and shares in computer firms.

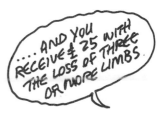

Alcohol and Tobacco Duty: These are put up in the annual ritual called the Budget. In essence, the idea is to stimulate trade at off-licences. After the January sales off-licences start putting up signs saying 'Beat the Budget!' and everyone flocks in to buy extra booze and fags, which are then consumed worrying about the details of the Chancellor's 'package for jobs' — as it is by hallowed tradition described.

Then fresh signs go up saying 'Pre-Budget prices while stocks last!' and everybody rushes out to get some more in.

These duties can be avoided by buying 'duty free' at airports etc. However this is a thoroughly irritating way of avoiding tax as you can never quite get out of your head the thought that you are still getting ripped off because whisky only costs about 10p a bottle to produce, and yet without tax it is *still* being knocked out at over a fiver a bottle.

Tax and PAYE

There is a joke which surfaces from time to time in comedians' acts, after-dinner speeches, humorous books etc., which suggests that there is to be a new tax form. Gone will be the familiar but highly complicated affair which currently exists, with its spaces for personal details, allowances, profits etc.

In its place will be a form with just three sections:

(1) How much did you earn last year?
(2) How much of it is left?
(3) Send it to us.

There's many a true word spoken in jest, but, it is as well to remember, quite a lot of old crap as well.

Anyone who is self-employed will immediately spot the flaw in this new form from the taxman's point of view. Indeed anyone who is self-employed would be only too delighted to have to pay in tax only what they have left at the end of the year, since that is usually zero or even less.

Self-employed people are required to pay tax on money they earn some time after they have earned it and usually just after they have spent it.

Their tax is dealt with under what is called 'Schedule D'. This is not too complicated. In fact it is as easy as Schedule A, B, C. The only problem for the Schedule D taxpayer is finding enough money this year to pay last year's tax.

This can prove difficult for pop stars, especially of the one-hit wonder variety, who earn millions of pounds with their chart-topping Eurosmash 'Boom Bang-A-Bang, I Love You Baby' and set about the business of getting rid of the money on gold Rolls Royces, groupies, roadies, toadies, agents, managers, country mansions, lines of coke, more groupies etc.

When the follow-up record 'Boom Love-A-Dove I Bang You Baby' unaccountably fails to repeat their previous success and the follow-down record 'Baby I Love Your Boom-Boom-Bang' barely scrapes into the charts, the trouble sets in.

From the Inland Revenue's point of view, a large sum of money is due on the year of 'Boom Bang-A-Bang', e.g. £500,000. However, since the stars are now reduced to busking on Underground Stations and playing Cambridge May Balls this can hardly be met out of current earnings.

The result is an appearance at the Bankruptcy Court (with no support).

Employed people are spared all this trouble (and also miss out on the Rolls Royces, groupies, lines of coke etc.), by being taxed under Schedule E and something called P.A.Y.E. (Pay As You Earn). Under this scheme tax is deducted from your pay packet at source. The word 'source' is used as the flow of money is thus reduced to a very small trickle. This means the government gets it immediately and you don't have a chance to fritter it away on luxuries like food, clothing etc.

In addition to P.A.Y.E. the employee has several other deductions to make from his pay packet, such as National Insurance and H.P. payments due on the furniture. The result is that his take-home pay (or T.A.K.E. H.O.M.E.P.A.Y. for short) frequently bears very little relation to his G.R.O.S.S. pay at all.

Here is a typical employee's monthly pay slip:

██

Name A. Typical Employee

Pay (basic)	£500.00
Overtime, bonus commission, productivity, profit share, extra, ex-gratia and adjustment payments	£ 5.00
GROSS PAY	£505.00

Deductions

Income Tax	£160.00
National Insurance	£ 80.00
Superannuation	£ 49.00
Union dues	£ 25.00
Social Club	£ 10.00
Christmas Club	£ 5.00
Cover charge	£ 1.00
VAT	£ 75.75
Service	£ 50.50
Parts	£ 98.00
Labour	£ 82.00
TOTAL DEDUCTIONS	£636.25

██

YOU OWE US £130.75. PLEASE PAY THIS SUM
IF YOU WISH TO REMAIN IN PAID EMPLOY-
MENT.

Scotsmen: An Apology

In response to accusations that Money Made Silly *has displayed a disparaging and patronising attitude to Scotsmen, we feel it's time we made it up to the wee little Jocks.*

Accordingly, we are pleased to print the text of a speech given by Sir David MacCabean of that Ilk, President of the Caledonian Friendship League, Edinburgh.

'It is traditional (explained Sir David) to regard the Scots as being mean with money. Why should such an open, generous and free-spending people be slandered in such a way? As a Scotsman myself I would give a hundred pence to anyone who can tell me.

Which reminds me of the Scotsman on a visit to Israel who complained about the price of the hire of boats on the Sea of Galilee.

"But," said the boatman, "this is no ordinary lake. This is the very water on which Jesus Christ walked."

"Well, no wonder he walked," replied the Scotsman. "Look at the price of the boats!"

Fellow Scotsmen, we must demonstrate that we can be as open-pursed as the next man, especially if he happens to be a Yorkshireman.

No more must we hear stories about the Aberdonian depressive who broke into his neighbour's house to gas himself to death.

And let us forget the joke about the Glaswegian tradesman who, hearing from his cousin that his warehouse was insured against fire, theft and earthquakes, remarked "Fire and theft I understand, but how do you arrange an earthquake?"

Particularly since this is a Jewish joke anyway.

It is time to stamp out such false and distorted images. We must launch a multi-media, world-wide campaign to enlighten people.

It will not be easy, but we in this society must do our best. It will not be inexpensive, but it must be done.'

At this point a collection for the speaker was announced, whereupon one member of the audience fainted and seven others carried him out.

Money Made

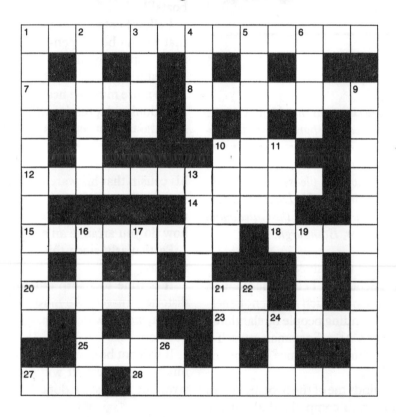

Silly Crossword

Across

1/ Someone in the pay office sounds like a foreign nobleman's employee. (8,5)

7/ 250 plus 80 plus one equals money abroad. (5)

8/ Given a shilling to force the newspaper man. (7)

10/ Valuable rock found in poor estates. (3)

12/ We want to go after a bit of leg in false hair and find a place to throw money away. (7,4)

14/ Communists expose overdrawn dollar. (4)

15/ Mashed neeps — and sex — should cover your outgoings. (8)

18/ One shilling from seven — that's not odd! (4)

20/ Generous payment being driven out in Gresham Street? (4,5)

23/ The doctor's first class hundred is being pieced together beautifully. (6)

25/ Right to hold on to something in Nile whirlpool. (4)

27/ Young aspiring professional is backward but fills a packet. (3)

28/ Author's payments for *The Old Man of Lochnagar*. (9)

Down

1/ Bill learning to confess. (11)

2/ Black birds with one point make money. (6)

3/ Peculiar ruse made by computer-operator. (4)

4/ Saliva put back for waiter. (4)

5/ The creed he put together gave joy. (7)

6/ Mixed up seer is Irish, or is it Scottish? (4)

9/ CND sections unplugs. (11)

10/ Nothing leaves three points in debt. (4)

11/ Shilling in a squirming eel, in another way. (4)

13/ Show us the colour of your money! (5)

16/ Post office in front of French airport makes you ill. (6)

17/ Song has no feeling before the Queen. (6)

19/ Six French companies make credit card. (4)

21/ Old girl's name for fifth letter shows that I am upside down over a graduate. (4)

22/ Heartless yahoo gives interjection. (2)

24/ Won after the game is over but before the match is over. (3)

26/ ⅖ths of 6s 8d. That can't be right! (2)

*Solution on p. 96

Doing Something Unusual and Writing a Book on It . .

The great thing about this way of getting rich is that there are so many different possibilities. Spending a year on a desert island without food or drink, climbing Everest in a pair of training shoes, having an interesting conversation with Richard Stilgoe . . . just as long as nobody's done it before and as long as you survive the ordeal and get back alive, you're made.

TV chat shows, *Start the Week* and opening jumble sales are just a few of the spin-offs that fall into your lap.

To make things easier, you don't even need to write the book yourself. As soon as you get back from your historic expedition, get yourself a decent agent and leave the rest to him.

Which reminds me . . .

£££££££££££££££££

Glossary

Nouveau riche   Very similar to nouvelle cuisine. Both are found in expensive restaurants, involve spending a lot of money and are extremely tasteless.

Tips   The Englishman's way of patronising someone who's been rude, offensive or given exceptionally bad service (see *Taxi Drivers Made Silly*).

Gratuity   Customer's way of tipping the waiter.

VAT   Taxpayer's way of tipping the government.

Bank holiday   Monday is traditionally the day for Bank Holidays, just as Tuesday is the day for the budget, Thursday for general elections, and Saturday the day when Arsenal disappoint their fans with a lack-lustre performance at gloomy Highbury Stadium.

Guinea   Old coin worth £1.05.

New Guinea   Country worth a visit.

Cheque guarantee cards   If a shopkeeper suspects that you have stolen the cheque book with which you propose to pay for goods, then production of the cheque guarantee card guarantees that you have stolen the card as well.

Automatic cash dispensers   Means that even after the bank is closed you can be told how big your overdraft is, and given some cash to make it even bigger. These clever machines were invented to save customers the misery of queuing in banks, and inflict on them the even greater misery of queuing in the High Street outside.

Pocket calculator   A useful device for preventing schoolchildren from learning how to do arithmetic.

Bank robbery   A method of queue-jumping in a bank involving guns, stockings, getaway cars etc.

Bank charges   See *Daylight robbery*.

Daylight robbery   A robbery of a Daylight Savings Bank.

'A basket of foreign currencies' Meaningless term used by the BBC when talking about the exchange rate, as in 'the pound fell to an all-time low when measured against a basket of foreign currencies.' Which currencies? What basket? Expressions like these are contained in a BBC phrasebook together with 'mainly Catholic SDLP', 'sources close to the Prime Minister', 'Israeli-backed Christian militiamen',

'chairman of the influential 1922 committee' etc. etc.

Gresham's Law   Gresham's Law states that bad money drives out good. So what?

Supply and demand   The one aspect of economics that everybody understands. It is encountered in most shops in Britain. Anything you ask a shopkeeper to supply, he'll say sorry, we don't stock them, there's no demand.

Keynesianism   Keynes' claim to fame is that during the 1920s and 1930s about 20% of the labour force was out of work, and he was one of the few people to notice it (apart from the unemployed themselves). His idea was to get the government to spend a lot of money to stimulate demand for goods and thus employ a lot of people. This approach was followed in Britain up to and after the war, until Margaret Thatcher realised that Keynesianism was the cause of galloping inflation, creeping socialism and Edward Heath.

Earnings-related pension scheme   Self explanatory. Government scheme soon to be abolished on the basis that by the year 2000 unemployment will be so high that there won't be any earnings to relate pensions to.

Midas   A legendary king who found that anything he touched turned to gold. Only man to win a gold medal at the Olympics by coming third. Inventor of Gold Top milk. Never known to masturbate.

Miras   Slightly less legendary king who found that anything he touched became tax-deductible.

Friendly Societies   Sort of financial institution. So called to distinguish them from banks.

BT   Ownership of shares in British Telecom entitles the holder to demand an answer to the age-old question as to why town codes aren't printed in the telephone directories instead of a little code book that you can never find when you most need it.

Legal tender   Money which it is compulsory to accept. Never a problem in Scotland.

Poverty trap   An expression to describe the complaints of a man with ten

children who can get more money from social security benefits, rent and rate rebates, supplementary allowances etc. than from actually doing any work, paying tax and so forth. After 20 years in the poverty trap such a man finds that his benefits start to drop off and he can't get a job because he is too old and hasn't got any experience. Shame. Still, serves him right for being such a lazy bugger in the first place.*

* This entry compiled by the Monday Club.

Inflation Inflation is the rocketing cost of, say, having your tyres pumped up.

It was at its worst in pre-war Germany when bank notes had so little value that people would carry them to the shops in a wheelbarrow to buy a loaf of bread, swap the wheelbarrow for the bread, and throw away the bank notes.

Since the Second World War inflation has become an established part of life in all Western countries and most of the Third World.

It can be blamed on excessive government expenditure, enlarged money supply, the Arabs, currency speculators, trade unions, profiteers, estate agents, politicians, the workers, the bosses, the gnomes of Zurich, the

Brauns of Zurich (bus-driver Klaus Braun and his wife and three children), the Left, the Right, Dr David Owen, Edward Heath, Harold Wilson, President Reagan, high wages, high prices, bad budgets, shopkeepers, middlemen, Middlesex, *Middlemarch* Terry Wogan, the BBC, the arms race, the Boat Race, *Any Questions*, Rupert Murdoch, tinkers, tailors, soldiers, sailors, Mabel the cat and everyone else at no. 39 who want to hear 'Tie a Yellow Ribbon' especially for Arthur who is 74 today.

£ £ WAYS OF GETTING RICH NO. 38(a) £ £

Marrying into the Royal Family . . .

Unfortunately there are only a limited number of opportunities for this desirable way of making your fortune, and although vacancies come up from time to time, entry is usually restricted to those who are already pretty well-heeled, e.g. the sons and daughters of the ruling aristocracy.

Try hanging around at the Badminton Horse Trials, keeping an eye on the classified ads in *Harpers & Queen*, or having your brain removed.

If you don't think you quite live up to the stereotype of a royal princess but still fancy a liaison with one of the royal princes, see WAYS OF GETTING RICH NO. 38(B), **Becoming an aspiring actress who gets picked up by Prince Andrew in a night club then flogs her story to one of the Sunday papers** . . .

£££££££££££££££££

Answers

Across: 1/Accounts clerk 7/Krone
8/Pressed 10/Ore 12/Wishing well
14/Reds 15/Expenses 18/Even 20/Good
money 23/Mosaic 25/Lien 27/Pay
28/Royalties

Down: 1/Acknowledge 2/Crowns
3/User 4/Tips 5/Cheered 6/Erse
9/Disconnects 10/Owes 11/Else
13/Green 16/Poorly 17/Number
19/Visa 21/Emma 22/Yo 24/Set 26/No